Britain in the Past
The Stone Age

Moira Butterfield

W

FRANKLIN WATTS

LONDON · SYDNEY

D0231882

Franklin Watts
First published in 2015 by the Watts Publishing Group

Copyright © The Watts Publishing Group 2015

All rights reserved.

Editor: Sarah Ridley
Editor in chief: John C. Miles
Series designer: Jane Hawkins
Art director: Peter Scoulding
Picture research: Diana Morris

Picture credits: AAA Collection/Alamy: 13t. Paul Avis/SPL: 7t. John Braid/Dreamstime: front cover, 24-25b. Clearview/Alamy: 11t. Cotswolds Photo Library/Alamy: 18b. Cresswell Crags: 9t. Mark Eaton/Dreamstime: 20c. English Heritage, Salisbury & S Wiltshire Museum/Bridgeman Art Library: 29b. Robert Estall photo agency/Alamy: 17t. Heritage Image Partnership/Alamy: 23t. © Historic England: 28b. Rita Manoj Jethani/Shutterstock: 27. Tomasz Kapala/Dreamstime: 26b. DaveKav/CC Wikipedia Commons: 8b. Erich Lessing/AKG Images: 23b. David Lyons/Alamy: 10b. Richard Melichar/Dreamstime: 16-17b. National Museum of Wales: 6c. The Trustees of the NHM, London: 5b. NHM, London/Alamy: 15t. NHM/Mary Evans PL : 7c. NHM, London courtesy of Rick Schulting: 19b. Pancaketom/Dreamstime: 19t. P Plailly/E Daynes/SPL: 5t. Courtesy of Salisbury Museum: 29t. Skyscan Photolibrary/Alamy: 22b. Paul D Stewart/SPL: 4b. Jens Stott/Dreamstime: 4tl, 6tl, 8tl, 10tl, 12tl, 14tl, 16tl, 18tl, 20tl, 22tl, 24tl, 26tl, 28tl. Tony Watson/Alamy:12b. Kevin Wheal/Alamy: 14c. Adam Woolfit/Corbis: 1, 21t.

Every attempt has been made to clear copyright. Should there be any inadvertent omission please apply to the publisher for rectification.

Dewey number: 941

Hardback ISBN: 978 1 4451 4051 3
Library eBook ISBN: 978 1 4451 4053 7

Printed in China

Franklin Watts
An imprint of
Hachette Children's Group
Part of The Watts Publishing Group
Carmelite House
50 Victoria Embankment
London EC4Y 0DZ

An Hachette UK Company
www.hachette.co.uk

www.franklinwatts.co.uk

Contents

Meet the first visitors   4

Find the first of our kind   6

Discover the first art   8

Go hunting and fishing   10

Meet a Mesolithic man   12

Plant the first crops   14

Honour the ancestors   16

Fight in the first battle   18

Sleep in a Stone Age bed   20

Crawl through a mine   22

Build a sacred circle   24

See the sun   26

Come to a winter feast   28

Glossary/Further information   30

Index   32

Meet the first visitors

The earliest humans in Britain lived in a time we call the Palaeolithic (*pay-leo-lithic*), meaning Old Stone Age, 2.5 million to 10,000 years ago. They looked very different to us and the countryside they lived in looked different, too.

First visitors

The first members of the human family came from Africa around 4.5 million years ago. We call them hominids. They looked more like chimps walking upright than modern humans. The oldest evidence we have for hominids in Britain are some stone tools made from flint, dating to around 750,000 years ago. They were found in Pakefield, Suffolk.

Boxgrove Man

The earliest human body part ever found in Britain was a piece of leg bone discovered in a quarry in Boxgrove, West Sussex. It belonged to a male who lived half a million years ago. We don't know what Boxgrove Man looked like, but we do know,

Look!

Early humans made tools for themselves by knapping, which means chipping at pieces of flint to make the ends pointed and the edges sharp. Here are some examples from around Britain.

◀ This imaginary picture of Boxgrove Man shows him carrying a wooden spear for hunting animals.

If you lived in the Stone Age...

Early Stone Age Britain was not an island. It was joined on to the rest of Europe and it was a much warmer place than it is today.
If you had been one of the first humans you would have lived amongst lions, hyenas, elephants and rhinos!

from his leg bone, that he was well-built and powerful, rather like a rugby player!

Swanscombe Woman

The first female found in Britain lived around 400,000 years ago. Three pieces of her skull were discovered in Swanscombe, Kent, and study of these bones proved that she belonged to a branch of the human family called Neanderthals. They were short and squat, with a brow that jutted out over the eyes.

This is part of the skull of Swanscombe Woman, the oldest known woman in Britain. ▼

Find the first of our kind

Modern-looking humans began to spread from Africa around 60,000 years ago. We know they were in Britain 33,000 years ago because we found one!

Mammoth hunter

Modern humans were taller and leaner than Neanderthals, with a different-sized brain. The skeleton of the earliest modern human we know of in Britain was discovered in Paviland Cave on the Gower Peninsula in Wales. He was a man in his twenties. He was probably a hunter-gatherer who roamed the

▲ There was probably some sort of ceremony when the Paviland hunter was buried.

land following animals such as reindeer and mammoths.

Buried treasures

We can tell from the man's burial that other people cared for him. He was buried with

▲ A human thigh bone,
stained with red ochre.

a necklace of tiny periwinkle
shells and some mysterious ivory
rods, rings and carved shapes.
Everything, including the man's
bones, was dyed red with a
type of coloured earth called
red ochre.

If you lived in the Stone Age...

Life would have been getting hard
for the Paviland hunter. There were
regular Ice Ages in Britain, when
the weather grew incredibly cold.
These were beginning to happen
in his lifetime.

Look!

The Reverend William Buckland
found the bones in 1823,
climbing down steep cliffs to
reach Paviland Cave. He thought
they came from a Roman woman
and he called her 'the red lady'.

How old?

We can pinpoint the date of
early bones such as the cave
skeleton by using radiocarbon
dating. All living things
contain a substance called
radioactive carbon. Over
time the radioactivity of the
carbon lessens bit by bit, and
it's possible to tell how old
something is by measuring how
much radioactivity is left.

Discover the first art

Around 12,000 years ago we know that bands of hunters were camping in Cresswell Caves in Nottinghamshire. They left the earliest British art behind.

Magical pieces

The art the hunters left behind includes an engraving of a horse on a piece of animal bone. Perhaps its owner thought it would magically help him with his hunting, but we can't be sure. At some point it was deliberately broken in half and scratched over.

Look in the middle of the rib bone to see the horse's head. This piece of art is about 12,500 years old. ▼

Look!

The engraved horse found at Cresswell Caves was made by a skilled artist, who beautifully captured the shape and movement of a horse leaping in a few simple lines. Modern artists such as Pablo Picasso were inspired by cave art like this.

▲ The long beak of a bird carved in the cave wall.

Wall work

The Cresswell Caves have the oldest examples of cave art found in Britain. Someone used a flint tool to carefully engrave the shapes of animals onto the rock, including birds, a bison and an ibex (a goat-like animal).

Left behind

Evidence shows that Ice Age hunters regularly stopped off in the Cresswell Caves for thousands of years, whenever the climate was warm enough for them to venture to Britain. They left all kinds of tools for cutting up and eating meat as well as a bone sewing needle.

If you lived in the Stone Age...

As a Palaeolithic person you might have worn jewellery such as shell necklaces and pendants made from animal teeth. It's thought that the tooth of a sabre-toothed cat, found at Cresswell Caves, may have come from a pendant.

Go hunting and fishing

Around 8000 BCE the last of the Ice Ages had disappeared and Britain had warmed up again. Forests of birch and elder trees grew up where there had once been thick ice and snow. Animals began to return from further south, and people followed them.

Welcome to the Mesolithic

The part of the Stone Age between 8000 BCE and 4000 BCE is called the Mesolithic *(mee-zo-lithic)*. We know that people hunted and gathered their food at this time. Mesolithic hunters set up camps and went fishing at Fiskary Bay on the Scottish Isle of Coll. They left behind tools, fish bones and roasted nuts.

If you lived in the Stone Age...

If you had lived in Mesolithic times you might have learnt to row a boat along a river or coastline. Part of a Mesolithic boat, carved from a log, has been found preserved underwater in the Solent near Southampton.

There were fish and shellfish to eat, and deer to hunt on Stone Age Coll. ▼

DIY guys

Mesolithic people had to be
practical to survive. They
made rope from deer sinews,
baskets from reeds and fish
harpoons from deer antlers.
They were skilled at making
microliths – tiny pieces of flint
worked into mini fishing barbs
and spear points.

The first address

The first permanent homes ever
found in Britain were built in
Mesolithic times. Archaeologists

Look!

Inside the Howick house there
were hearths and nutshells.
Somebody had been roasting tasty
hazelnuts on a fire there. This is a
modern reconstruction (above).

found evidence of one at Star
Carr in Yorkshire (from around
11,500 years ago) and another
at Howick in Northumberland
(from around 11,000 years ago).
Both houses were round, with
wooden posts like a wigwam.
They would have been covered
in animal skins and thatch.

Meet a Mesolithic man

The oldest complete skeleton ever found in Britain belonged to a Mesolithic man who died around 9,000 years ago. It was discovered in Gough's Cave, Cheddar, Somerset.

▲ The skeleton of Cheddar Man in his cave.

If you lived in the Stone Age...

It's possible that if you were a Mesolithic hunter like Cheddar Man you may have worn a deer skull mask to perform magical hunting rituals. A deer skull mask was found in Star Carr, Yorkshire, dating from 7500 BCE.

Hunter's home

Cheddar Man lived around 7000 BCE. We know he died in his twenties, perhaps from an infection that caused the hole in the front of his skull. There were other even older human bones in the cave, suggesting that people sheltered there up to 14,700 years ago, straight after the last Ice Age. Like them, Cheddar Man would have been a hunter. There were butchered animal bones in the cave, too.

Cannibal cave

Some of the human bones found in the cave had been butchered, pointing to cannibalism. We don't know if this was done as part of a religious ritual after someone's death, or just because of hunger.

A modern relation

Scientists were able to extract DNA from Cheddar Man's bones. Adrian Targett, a teacher living in Cheddar, turned out to be Cheddar Man's descendant, proving that Adrian's ancestors had been living in the West Country for 9,000 years and had Mesolithic relatives!

Look!

Using Cheddar Man's skull, experts reconstructed a model of his head (above). You can see his skeleton and the reconstruction of his head at the Natural History Museum in London.

Plant the first crops

Around 6,000 years ago people arrived in Britain from Europe, bringing the first seeds of grain to plant and farm. This led to a completely new way of life.

The first farmers

People began to clear patches of forest to grow crops, and they began to keep farm animals such as cattle. We call this era the Neolithic *(nee-oh-lithic)*.

The stones we see at Coldrum, Kent, were once covered in a mound of earth and formed a tomb for the dead. ▼

Instead of following animals, families began to settle in one place. One of the first tombs in Britain was built by some of the very first farmers, at Coldrum in Kent, around 4000 BCE.

If you lived in the Stone Age...

If you were part of a Neolithic farming family you would have lived on land cleared of trees. The wildwood would not have been far away though, where red deer, elk, boars and bears still lived.

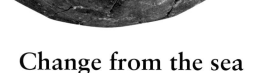

Look!

The very first pottery appeared at the same time as the first farms. People needed pots to store the food they were growing and making.

This Neolithic pot was found in Avebury, Wiltshire. ▶

A harder life

Archaeologists working at Coldrum found the bones of 22 people in the stone tomb, ranging from babies up to people in their forties. Their bones show that they were less healthy than hunters from earlier times because their diet was poorer and they had to work harder to prepare their food. They ground grain on stones to make flour, and the long hours of hard work wore out their backbones. The gritty flatbread cooked from the flour wore their teeth down.

Change from the sea

The Neolithic people who brought grain, farming tools, sheep and cows to Britain must have transported them by boat. We know this because Britain became an island around 6100 BCE, when a huge landslide in the area of Norway triggered a gigantic tsunami. Towering 10m-high waves tore across low-lying areas, engulfing the land between Britain and Europe.

Honour the ancestors

Now families were staying put, their numbers increased. That meant there were more people in Britain, and groups began to lay claim to land. High up on hilltops they built stone tombs for their dead, and probably for their neighbours to see, too.

Built for show

Neolithic people buried some of their relatives in long barrows – specially-built stone chambers covered on top with earth. Over 300 Neolithic long barrows have survived in Britain. One of the best-preserved examples is the West Kennet long barrow in Wiltshire. It was built 5,600 years ago, and is 100m long and 20m wide. It could be seen for miles around.

▼ The entrance to the long barrow is on the left, by the big stones.

Look!

The West Kennet long barrow had sarsen stones dragged up to the entrance. Sarsen stones are big sandstone boulders found lying on the ground in some parts of the country. Stone Age builders often used them for tombs and stone circles (see p24).

House of the dead

Inside the dark shadowy long barrow there were five chambers leading off a long corridor. Bones from 36 or more people were laid in the different chambers over a period of about 25 years. The bones were carefully arranged in the chambers and there is evidence that feasts were held outside.

A murder mystery?

We don't know how people were chosen to be buried in the long barrow. The only complete skeleton belonged to an elderly man. He had a broken arm and there was a flint arrowhead embedded in his skeleton. He may have been killed violently but we can't tell for sure.

▲ Inside the long barrow there were rooms for the bones, rather like a house for the dead.

If you lived in the Stone Age...

If you lived in a Neolithic community you might have helped to build a long barrow. Archaeologists estimate it took nearly 16,000 man-hours to build West Kennet, so lots of people must have worked together to complete it.

Fight in the first battle

Groups of people began to fight each other in Neolithic times, probably for land. The first battle we know of took place around 5,500 years ago on Crickley Hill in Gloucestershire.

The defenders

A farming community lived on top of the hill. They had homes inside a circular ditch, with two gaps called causeways for letting people and animals in and out. At some point they must have sensed danger because they erected a high wooden fence called a palisade around the ditch, with gates at the entrances.

People lived on top of Crickley Hill, but attackers arrived from below. ▼

Look!

Arrowheads at this time were leaf-shaped and were beautifully made from delicate pieces of flint.

The attackers

In 3500 BCE the settlement was attacked from below by enemies carrying lethal wooden longbows. The remains of 450 flint arrowheads have been found, mostly pointing up the hill. The arrowheads were glued onto wooden shafts using pine resin. Fired from a longbow, they could go through a body up to 30m away.

Winners and losers

Most of the arrowheads were going one way, so this may have been an ambush. It seems the attackers won because the palisade and the gates were burnt down, along with the homes inside. We have no idea what happened to the losers.

If you lived in the Stone Age...

If you lived in Neolithic Britain at this time you would have needed to watch out for enemies. Lots of skulls have been found around southern Britain dating from the same time as the Crickley Hill battle and showing injuries from heavy blows. It seems there was lots of fighting.

Holes in these Neolithic skulls are evidence of a violent death. ▼

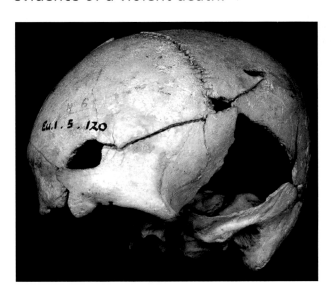

Sleep in a Stone Age bed

At Skara Brae on mainland Orkney, Scotland you can visit a very rare site – the remains of eight Neolithic homes built around 5,000 years ago.

If you lived in the Stone Age...

If you lived in Skara Brae 5,000 years ago, you would have slept on a stone bed with straw as a mattress and some animal skin blankets to keep you warm.

Look!

Some mysterious carved stone balls, about the size of pine cones, were found at Skara Brae. Perhaps they were used for ceremonies or for games. Some tiny ivory gaming dice were also found on the site.

Stone homes

The Skara Brae homes were built from stone, with turf on the roofs. Everything inside the houses was stone (see left). There was a stone hearth for a fire, stone beds around the walls and a set of stone shelves like a modern dresser. Some of the homes even had stone tanks where they kept live limpets for food and fish bait.

Bone and stone treasures

So many bone beads have been found at Skara Brae that archaeologists have wondered if jewellery was being made there. A fine carved bone necklace was found, too, along with bone hair pins. Some beautiful but puzzling carved stone balls were also left behind (see above). We don't know what they were for.

Ancient rubbish

Once people began to stay in one place they began to leave piles of rubbish! The inhabitants of Skara Brae left behind trash heaps called middens, including the remains of their meals. We know from their middens that they ate fish, shellfish, cattle and sheep. They grew wheat and hunted animals such as red deer.

Crawl through a mine

Neolithic people used flint tools, particularly polished axes with wooden handles that enabled them to cut down trees for farmland. At Grimes Graves in East Anglia the flint was mined from deep down in the earth.

Digging deep

The mines at Grimes Graves were shafts dug down into the chalk rock to reach the best flint, around 15m below. From 3000 BCE onwards, people dug 430 shafts using picks and shovels made from antler and ox bones. Today, the shafts look like round shapes in the ground.

Dark and dangerous

Wooden ladders led down the shafts to the darkness below. At the bottom, tunnels led sideways into the rock, some so tiny that only children could have worked in them. The miners left pottery, animal and human skulls in the mines. Perhaps they were used in some kind of ceremony.

These dimples in the ground mark the old mine site. ▼

If you lived in the Stone Age...

If you lived at Grimes Graves you and your family would probably be digging in the mines or making flint tools above ground. You would be one of the first industrial workers in Britain, making goods that were probably traded with other people around the country.

It must have required a team effort to get the flint from underground. ▶

The best axes

Neolithic farmers used axes to cut down trees, but the Grimes Graves miners were producing something extra special. They mined a particularly black and shiny flint called floorstone, which made very impressive-looking axes. These were probably highly-prized and perhaps owned by the most important people in a community. Such fine axes were probably used for ceremonies, not for work.

Look!

The beautiful Neolithic axehead on the left is made of polished jade and might have been used in ceremonies. It was found in Canterbury, Kent, but made in the Italian Alps. It shows that people were travelling in Neolithic times, bringing objects from far away.

Build a sacred circle

Five thousand years ago impressive stone circles and burial mounds began to appear around the country. Some of the finest examples can be seen on mainland Orkney.

A mystery landscape

The Neolithic people of Orkney spent years building a vast stone circle called the Ring of Brodgar, setting up around 60 stones inside a huge ditch. Further along in the landscape there is another stone circle called the Stones of Stenness, and nearby there is a massive mound with a passage running through it, called Maeshowe passage tomb.

Winter sun secret

Maeshowe was very skilfully built. Its narrow stone passage leads to a stone chamber 12m high, and for a few days in midwinter the setting sun shines down the passageway and lights up the chamber. We don't know

The Ring of Brodgar, an ancient stone circle on Orkney. ▼

whose bones were put into the tomb, but we do know that the ritual of the midwinter sun was important enough for people to spend a lot of effort building the tomb in just the right place.

Sacred places

It seems as though the stone circles and the Maeshowe tomb were somehow connected. Archaeologists call this type of area a 'sacred landscape', because it has several different features that must have been important to people's beliefs.

New work on the site has revealed even more Neolithic features, such as buildings and a man-made mound.

If you lived in the Stone Age...

If you had lived around 5,000 years ago you might have taken part in ceremonies at stone circles, perhaps led by early priests of some kind.

See the sun

The most famous British ancient monument of all, Stonehenge in Wiltshire, shows us that in Neolithic times people began to believe in cosmology, which means they believed in some kind of link between the sky and the Earth.

If you lived in the Stone Age...

The site around Stonehenge is a giant sacred landscape. There were once other wooden circles, ditches, mounds and a giant causeway called a cursus. People living in the area knew it was a very important religious place.

Sparkly stones

Stonehenge began as a circular ditch with a ring of wooden posts inside it. Then, around 5,500 years ago, a great effort was made to bring some special stones all the way from south-west Wales to build a stone circle. They are called bluestones because they are a blue-green colour, and they sparkle with tiny silver pieces when they are wet.

Bigger and grander

Stonehenge changed over time. The bluestones were moved and big sarsen stones were brought in to make a new circle. We don't know why people decided to change the monument. Perhaps they wanted to make it look grander for their ceremonies, probably held at the summer and winter solstices – the longest and shortest days of the year.

Ceremony of light

The stones of Stonehenge are placed so that they line up

Look!

People were cremated (burnt) or buried near Stonehenge, and we know from bone studies that one of the buried men was killed by arrows. He may have been sacrificed, but we can't know for sure.

with the rays of the sun at particular times of year. When the sun rises at the summer or winter solstice, it shines directly between the stones into the centre of the circle.

◀ It would have been hard work to move and position all the heavy stones.

Come to a winter feast

Around 4,500 years ago, at Durrington Walls near Stonehenge, there was a large circle made of wooden posts, near a Neolithic village. It seems that big parties were held there!

Winter party

From rubbish left behind on the site we know that 4,000 or more Neolithic people came to the wooden circles at Durrington Walls at midwinter for rituals and a big feast. They may have cremated (ceremonially burnt) the remains of dead relatives at the site and then taken the remains for burial around Stonehenge.

If you lived in the Stone Age...

In late Neolithic times you might have come to Durrington Walls with your family, then walked up to Stonehenge to take part in rituals remembering dead ancestors. Like many secrets of the Stone Age, nobody knows for sure!

Look!

Hundreds of arrowheads have been found at Durrington. Perhaps animals were ritually hunted there before being cooked for the feast. This pig bone was found with an arrowhead embedded in the top.

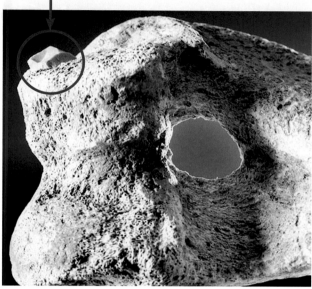

Hunt and hog roast

Cattle and pig teeth from 80,000 animals have been found at Durrington. We can tell from the teeth that the animals were born in spring, fattened up and then killed when they were nine months old. That's how we know that the Durrington feasting went on in winter.

The Stone Age ends

A type of pottery called groove-ware has been found at Durrington. It came originally from Orkney, and it shows that people and goods were travelling around Britain. Soon travellers would bring a new product to Britain and change the way people lived forever. Around 2500 BCE the first metal objects arrived and the Stone Age gave way to a new era that we call the Bronze Age.

▼ This pot from the time is called groove-ware because of the way it has been decorated by the potter.

29

Glossary

Cannibalism When humans eat the flesh of other humans.

Causeway enclosure A village inside a circular ditch and bank, with a couple of entrances.

Cremation When a dead body is burnt in a ritual ceremony.

DNA A chemical pattern like a signature, found in living cells and passed on to you by your ancestors.

Floorstone A type of black and shiny flint.

Groove-ware A type of pottery made in late Neolithic times.

Hominid A member of the human species, but not necessarily a modern human.

Hunter-gatherer Someone who hunts wild animals and gathers wild food to eat.

Ice Age A period of time when there was a very cold climate.

Knapping Shaping pieces of flint to make tools.

Long barrow A long stone tomb built under a mound. Inside there was a tunnel and chambers where bones were placed.

Mesolithic The time between 8000 BCE and 4000 BCE. It means Middle Stone Age.

Microlith A tiny piece of flint made into a tool such as a fishing barb or a spear point.

Neanderthal A branch of the human family found in Britain around 400,000 years ago.

Neolithic The time from 4000 BCE to 2500 BCE. It means New Stone Age.

Ochre A reddish-coloured earth.

Palaeolithic The time between 2.5 million and 10,000 years ago. It means Old Stone Age.

Radiocarbon dating Finding out the age of something by measuring its radioactive carbon.

Wildwood Huge area of natural forest that once grew in Europe.

Further information

Weblinks

http://www.creswell-crags.org.uk/
Discover the world of Ice Age hunters and see lots of the things they left behind.

http://www.english-heritage.org.uk/daysout/properties/stonehenge/?lang=en
Take a virtual tour of Stonehenge. See a Neolithic house reconstruction and look at some of the Stone Age treasures found in the area.

http://www.scottishten.org/property3
Take a virtual tour through the chambered tomb of Maeshowe on Orkney.

http://www.orkneyjar.com/history/skarabrae/
Pay an online visit to the Neolithic settlement of Skara Brae.

Note to parents and teachers: Every effort has been made by the Publishers to ensure that the web sites in this book are suitable for children, that they are of the highest educational value, and that they contain no inappropriate or offensive material. However, because of the nature of the Internet, it is impossible to guarantee that the contents of these sites will not be altered. We strongly advise that Internet access is supervised by a responsible adult.

Timeline

5–4.5 million years ago The first members of the human family appear in Africa.

500000 BCE The date of the first human-type remains ever found in Britain.

24000 BCE The date of the first modern-style human remains found in Britain.

11000 BCE The rough date of the first art discovered in Britain.

10000 BCE The end of the last Ice Age in Britain.

9000 BCE The date of the first dwelling found in Britain.

7000 BCE The date of the first complete human skeleton found in Britain.

6100 BCE A giant tsunami cuts Britain off from Europe.

4000 BCE Around the time when the first farmers grow crops in Britain.

3600 BCE Around the time when long barrows are built in Britain.

2550 BCE Stones were added to Stonehenge, which was previously a ring of wooden posts.

2500 BCE Bronze arrives in Britain.

Index

Africa 4, 6
arrowheads 17, 19, 29
art 8–9
axes 22–23

barrows, long 16–17
battles 18–19
beliefs 24–27
boats 10, 15
bones 4–9, 12–17, 19, 21–22, 25, 27
Boxgrove Man 4–5
Bronze Age 29
Buckland, Rev. William 7
burials 6, 14–17, 24–28

cannibalism 13
ceremonies 6, 21–23, 25–29
Cheddar Man 12–13
circles, stone 16, 24–27
climate 5, 7, 9–10
Coldrum 14
cosmology 26–27
Cresswell Caves 8–9
Crickley Hill battle 18–19

dating, radiocarbon 7
diet 9–11, 15, 21, 29
Durrington Walls 28–29

farming 14–15, 18, 21–23
feasts 17, 28–29

fishing 10–11
flints 4, 9, 11, 17, 19, 22–23
forests 10, 14, 22

Grimes Graves 22–23

hominids 4–5
houses 11–12, 18, 20–21
Howick 11
hunters/hunting 5–11, 13, 15, 21, 29

Ice Ages 7, 9–10, 13
Isle of Coll 10

jewellery 7, 9, 21

landscape, sacred 24–27

Maeshowe passage tomb 24–25
mammoths 6
Mesolithic 10–13
middens 21
mines 22–23
mounds, burial 24–26

Neanderthals 5–6
Neolithic 14–29
Norway 15

Orkney 20–21, 24–25, 29

Palaeolithic 4–9
palisades 18–19
Paviland hunter 6–7
pottery 15, 22, 29

Ring of Brodgar 24–25
rituals 12–13, 28

Skara Brae 20–21
solstices 24–25, 27
Star Carr 11–12
Stonehenge 26–28
stones, sarsen 16, 27
Stones of Stenness 24–25
Swanscombe Woman 5

tombs 14–17, 24–25
tools 4, 9–11, 15, 22–23
trade 23, 29
tsunami 15

waste pits 21, 28
weapons 5, 11, 17, 19, 23
West Kennet long barrow 16–17
wildlife 5–6, 8–10, 14
wildwood 14